MANAGEMENT FROM HEART

INSPIRATIONS VOLUME 1

ANIL KUMAR BHATIA

www.whitefalconpublishing.com

Management From Heart
Anil Kumar Bhatia

www.whitefalconpublishing.com

All rights reserved
First Edition, 2022
© Anil Kumar Bhatia, 2022
Cover design by White Falcon Publishing, 2022
Cover image source freepik.com/pixabay.com

No part of this publication may be reproduced, or stored in a retrieval system, or transmitted in any form by means of electronic, mechanical, photocopying or otherwise, without prior written permission from the author.

The contents of this book have been certified and timestamped on the POA Network blockchain as a permanent proof of existence. Scan the QR code or visit the URL given on the back cover to verify the blockchain certification for this book.

The views expressed in this work are solely those of the author and do not reflect the views of the publisher, and the publisher hereby disclaims any responsibility for them.

Requests for permission should be addressed to
consultanil18566@gmail.com

ISBN - 978-1-63640-607-7

MANAGEMENT FROM HEART

Inspirations Volume 1

MFH speaks

"Life, business and management are simple but not easy. They require our full time and dedication. In our attempt to make them easy, we complicate them."

> "The unison of heart and head. Head, heart and guts are all blended together to form one brain."

"Everybody is a leader;

this is for everybody & this is for the leader."

> "We are all together, we are all complementing, we are all interdependent and we are simply co-existing..."

> "How sincere are we with recruitment?
> We do more groundwork when it is a matter of buying a car for our office than for hiring a person."

Strengthen the process of recruitment

"Don't focus on the people, focus on the recruitment process; training, upgrading, retaining and providing a happy atmosphere."

> *"There are few critical relationships where we should be more polite, more human, but...*
> *we often ignore them; these are subordinates, neighbors, spouse...*
> *Why? I don't know."*

> "Every person in this world is a Manager or,
> a better word, Leader,
> this is how GOD made us."

"The king should never be blind. He has to use his own eyes to see the situation... Always."

> "I have been very fond of reading and a strong believer that we can learn a lot from other people's experiences which come to us from reading."

"I am astonished at the management skills, versatility and management capabilities of my mother and my wife."

MFH says

"Don't focus on controlling, focus on the process. It is the only controller..."

"Competition kills team work and team spirit; never allow it to enter your organization..."

"Developing relationship precedes communication. Communication effectiveness is in direct relation to your relationship..."

"Business and human management are in no way related to war and sports, it is life and has to be lived. It is not a competition and it is not an event.

It is a perennial, never ending commitment."

AB-MFH

"Repetition brings excellence..."
AB-MFH

> "Nothing comes in life easy. Management is about increasing the comfort zone of individual team members. It is as simple as parenting, definitely not easy."

"Life, business and management are not about competition. Let competition remain in sports. We are for interdependence and co-existence..."

> "A calm person does not pretend to be busy when everybody is under stress to pretend that they are busy..."

MFH believes –

> "Most of the actions which get appreciation and results are based on creativity of a few followed by a very, very long period of consistency by many."

"I must ask... ask... and ask,
and still if the job is not done
then ask again.
This is the only difference between
a good manager and
a not-so-good manager."

> "That's the answer to my quest for management principles.
>
> My HOME is where I have to seek solutions to all my problems, including management."

"A true leader never leads.

A true leader gives chance to his team members to take the lead and become leaders. They are available as a backup support, just in case..."

> *"Organizations which are personified tend to develop more belongingness..."*
> AB-MFH

"We all know that we cannot learn cycling by reading books & manuals and attending theory classes. We have to practice and practice with real equipment till we master it.

But, in practical life, business and management, we simply read or listen to a concept and go out to implement it.
Result is...?"

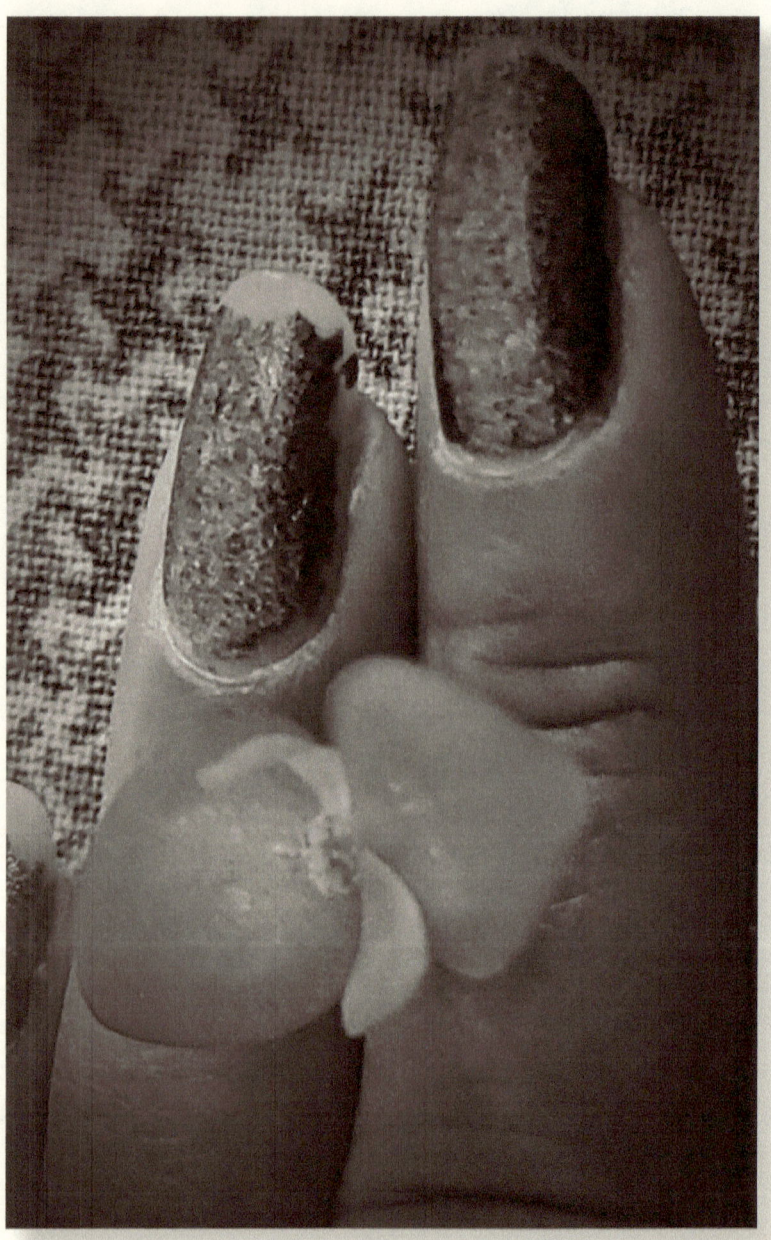

"The biggest non-sense statement which is commonly used is: I will take help once I have everything under control." **AB-MFH**

> CHANGE**, MFH** says-
>
> "You only have to demonstrate that the changes proposed are good for the **organization**. People can go to any extent to make **their** organizations great.
>
> Last but not the least, make changes comfortable..."

FOCUS ON THE PROCESS

"The success mantra of all successful organizations is their focus on

continuously improving the processes.

Growth and participation in this process of continuous improvement are the biggest motivation any management can provide..."

AB-MFH

"I have the spectator's view and he has the player's view. Yes.

That's the difference between the two of us. What he missed as a player, I realized as a spectator even without knowing the subject well."

> *"If your head, heart and guts are well blended with the brain, which is in its right place,*
> *you will never have to bite your tongue…"*

"My experience is in contradiction to modern thinking which advocates,

"Do what you like."

The better version could be,

"Do what you are successful at…"

AB-MFH

MFH reveals

"Interview-giving is a skill.

Nowadays, there are a number of centers which train people in this skill.

I have to decide,

I need people with good interview skills or good in the skills required to perform well in their jobs..."

> *"Wisdom is the difference between highly qualified and well qualified..."*

MFH makes us aware

"We can achieve much more than what we can visualize, calculate or plan based on our knowledge today...

History confirms that we are often restricted by our knowledge and awareness."

AB-MFH

"People can do wonders if they have a confidant, an ear that can listen to them without being judgmental."

CO-EXISTENCE

"Nature is a combination of highly interdependent existences who cannot thrive without each other,

which are continuously providing and receiving sustenance material from each other to exist together, at the same time in the same place.

A realistic combination of independence and interdependence is called **coexistence.**"

---

*"If you want people to be happy,
show and acknowledge their success.
Make their success happen."*

AB-MFH

"We cannot ignore the fact that people can be overshadowed by their seniors and parents...

The onus of my subordinate's behavior lies more on me than on them.

It's a real issue."

> "Following management tools are available to make a business perennial:
> - *continuous de-bottlenecking,*
> - *expanding, and*
> - *trusting..."*

MFH success guarantee steps;

1. Develop 'faith' in my purpose.
2. Develop 'faith' in my process.
3. Faith is 0% or 100%, even 99.9 is 0.

These simple steps are guarantee to my success.

Simple but not easy...

MFH asks -

"Have we got the guts and will power to create a **control-free** organization with only Doers and Providers?"

> **IMPORTANCE OF COMMENTATORS:**
>
> "The commentators have a very special role. They are supposed to create a vision of what is happening on the field for the spectators who are not present physically on the field.
>
> Visualize a commentator's role and importance because your views about the event are going to be based on his capabilities and honesty."

"Stop thinking what you like and start doing what you are successful at. You will be happy and satisfied..."
AB-MFH

AB-MFH

"A small creativity, to be useful,

needs to be followed by a long, long slog of unsung consistency."

> **"Comfort is the largest and fastest selling commodity** but something bigger than this motivates people to do great jobs like scaling peaks, competitive events, entrepreneurship, etc. This something extra is steered by the feeling of success. Motivation for it comes from within but managements have a big role here."

THE MISSING CONTROL FUNCTION

"In life, business and management, there are only two types of functions:
Line functions and support functions.
But we are always running the non-existent third function, the control function."

"Every day I tell myself – I love you..."
AB-MFH

> "Data is a dumb collection of numbers which has the potential to change the world when combined with statistical analysis and common sense."

"We have to re-design the jobs and job-evaluation in such a way that all team members are in control of their earnings on a real-time basis."

> **THE YES MANAGER**
>
> "I have a simple method of management. I simply say YES to everything that my team members bring to me.
>
> The results are simply wonderful..."

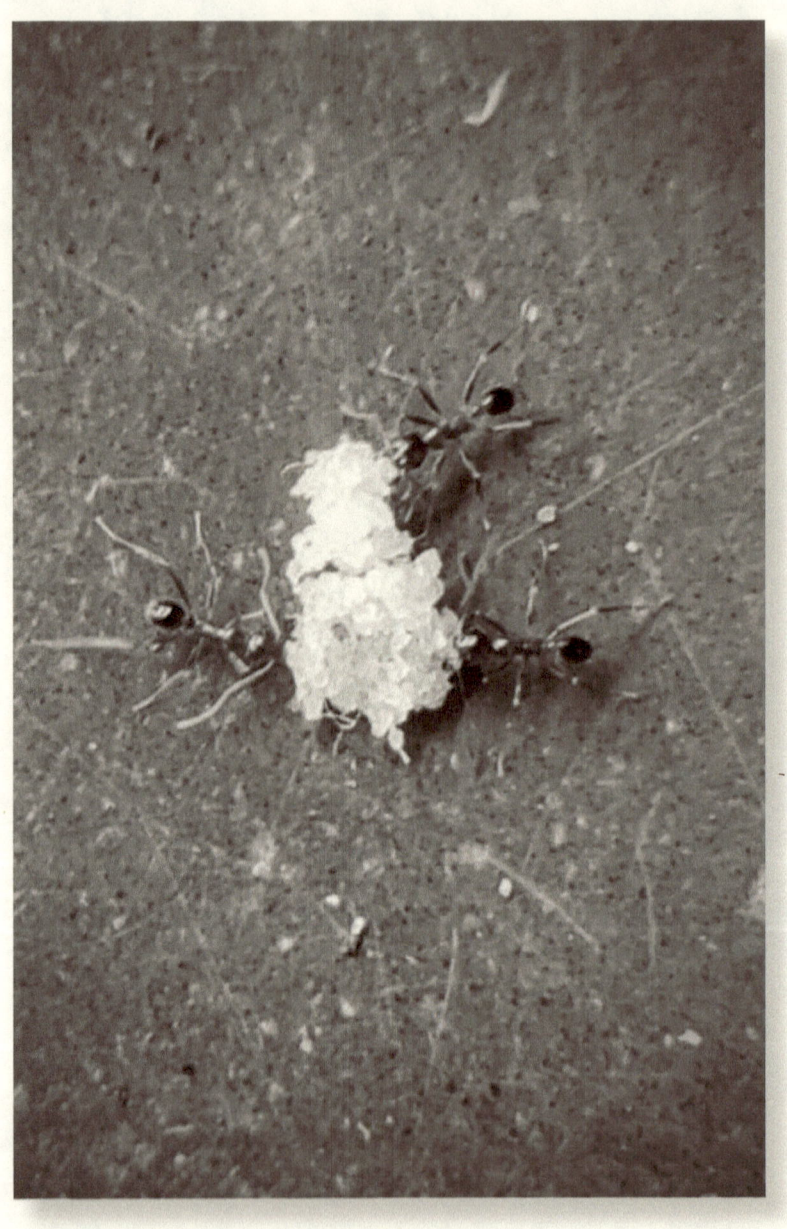

> NEVER HAVE A **BLIND** HEAD
>
> "The head or the main decision taker cannot be blind in any organization. He has to use all his faculties to gage the information."

"I have also remarked that video conferencing is more popular than con-calls (available for quite some time) because people communicate more visually than words." **AB-MFH**

> "Work energizes and tension tires..."
> **AB-MFH**

"From the time we are born, we are trained to be a wrestler, an individual sport, from kindergarten to primary to college...

And in organizations, we are expected to play football, a team game.

All managements should be aware of this."

Basis of MANAGEMENT FROM HEART

"Efficient self-management of mothers, wives, fathers and husbands is the basis of MFH. The case of mothers and wives is more important because they are mostly unsupervised and self-driven, thus proving the point."

> *"Tame your EGO, you can do wonders..."*
> **AB-MFH**

"You get the best analysis of a situation when you put yourself in the spectators' seat and come out of the players' shoes."

> "Vision should never be obscured by petty targets and targets are always petty.
>
> You can always achieve better than the best targets that you fix..."

"When we are working with humans,
remember it is individuality and
in-comparability..."
AB-MFH

> **MFH warns**
>
> "Is it a conflict situation which we are trying to avoid behind perception?
>
> In life, business and management we should talk about facts.
>
> If one person says it is 6 & another 9,
>
> we cannot say both are correct.
>
> The truth is one – either 6 or 9."

"Continuous de-bottlenecking
is much more vital.
It is more difficult too,
as it needs introspection; a difficult job."

MFH on THE LEARNING PROCESS

"Three years ago, I realized that from the last 30 years what I thought I was learning was, in fact, simply reading.

I learn only when I teach my team members and am able to guide them to implement the same, or

if I am able to directly implement the same.

Only then my reading becomes my learning...

> *"Organization is a garden of a variety of co-existent species of plants..."*

MFH introduces DT (Decision Taking)

"This is one of the important distinctions that needs to be understood in life, business and management.

There are three distinct activities

1. Problem solving
2. Decision making &
3. Decision taking."

"How can any business sustain?

The only way is growth.

How can a business grow?

There are only two ways -

De-bottlenecking & Expansion.

Both have to go simultaneously, hand in hand."

> **MFH** submits that
> *"Belongingness is one factor that has taken the biggest hit by the wrong interpretation of the word professionalism..."*

"Most of the organizational inefficiencies stem from:

Either an attempt to acquire the control function, or

an attempt to control the non-controllables."

MFH on

Who is the leader?
"The first person who gets a job done by a group of persons is the leader."

> "Self-assessment is impossible to be done by self.
>
> MFH believes that it is a misnomer, a difficult-to-digest fact.
>
> Be sure, invariably we need a confidant for proper Self-assessment."

MFH believes

"Life, business and management are always being in a state of continuity.

A series of growth steps big & small.

The prospects and potential are limitless.

Putting restrictions limits the horizons & the possibilities of expansion."

MFH – THE MANAGEMENT LESSON

"Do you want your team members to share or hide information, especially the unpleasant ones?

Do you want that small issues be hidden till they become expensive burdens?

Do you expect that a daily report, a weekly report and a monthly follow up will serve the purpose of controlling?"

> ***TARGETS ARE LIMITING:*** *"Was it possible to move from 100watt incandescent lamp to 8watt LED by setting TARGETS?"*

MAJORITY CANNOT GUARANTEE THE RIGHT

"Democratic decision taking (DT) has been proved to be an incomplete method.

It suits people who are not capable of taking the responsibility & accountability of their decision and are searching for an escape route..."

"If animals can be humane to each other,
If we can be humane to animals,
If we can be humane to strangers...
Why are we not humane with our:
Neighbors
Peers
Subordinates
Team members...?"

> "Don't give annual and performance-linked increments. Always keep the remuneration of the team members as per their individual market value." **AB-MFH**

"We cannot expect to bring any positive
change by continuously
showing,
discussing and
highlighting the negative."

MFH on HIRING OF SPECIALISTS

Yes, an idea can come from anyone, novice to specialist, associated to non-associated.

Involving specialists for implementation of the idea can save time and energy.

BUT

"There are two types of specialists:

One with years of experience, or

One with experience of years.

Choose the specialist carefully."

> *"Behind every successful person is one person who showed trust in the person.*
>
> *Can you be that one person for your team members?*
>
> *Can you be that top management which encourages the Managers, Leaders, Executives of your organization to be that one person?"*

"Targets are growth deterrent, thinking restrictor, waste generator, individualistic, limiting, insensitive;
be aware."

> "First, we set low targets & then we get contented with 90% achievement. Targets are limiting & retarding."

"Patience is a virtue

Is an incomplete statement...

Patience and impatience both are great virtues.

MFH does not consider these qualities as antonyms, they are independent qualities.

Be flexible, be situational."

> *"Work energizes and tension tires. Target is an energy drainer as it gives tension."*

"Our assessment about our team is so misleading that we end up hiring the wrong person for training, coaching or guiding our leaders." **AB-MFH**

> "Planning needs to be alive and dynamic, but that is against the conventional thinking which treats a plan as a fixed roadmap..."

"Creativity is also simple like other great things. It does not imply inventing 'A'.

It is utilizing the knowledge of one field for the benefit of the other..."

> "Time is the only asset that is equally distributed to each one of us, every day, every time. Make the best use of your 24 hours today..."

*"The Management that doubts the sincerity of the team members,
needs to introspect..."* **AB-MFH**

> "I always thought that people don't want
> to leave their comfort zones,
> but I was wrong.
> In fact, the opportunity to leave the
> so-called comfort zone, without disturbing
> the family compulsions and needs, is a big
> motivation booster."

DON'T FOCUS ON SALES

"Focus on the process of making
the right product,
pricing it right,
reaching the right customer and
the process of providing happy possession to
the customer."

TARGETS LEAD TO COMPROMISES

On a TV show - a competition for making cakes. A rack of utensils, cooking systems, rack of ingredients & whatever is required for the job.
A time limit of 40 minutes.

I was surprised to see that most of the time the contestant who focussed on time ended up losing because of either -

making some irreparable error or

by not being able to cook the dish in time.

Most often, the contestants who made moderate, just-a-cake won.

Those who tried to make excellent cakes were not able to finish in time. The best-to-be products usually got messed up during the last few minutes under pressure of time.

The winners were usually those who compromised on quality, finesse and required detailing.

"Self-assessment is nearly impossible..."
AB-MFH

> "Multitasking implies doing several tasks at a time. It does not imply doing many tasks together.
>
> It involves handling a large number of tasks,
>
> in breaks, one after another like we handled our subjects in our schools..."

"Managements need to understand that leadership also needs to be managed and it is very important.

Unmanaged leadership can be damaging & dangerous.

Simple but not easy..."

> "Leadership is all about learning, teaching, de-learning & re-learning for teaching..."

MFH says

*"As in life, in business and management too, **intention** is the most important factor. Any action receives its response based upon the intention of the action."*

> **LET POSITIVITY RULE**
>
> "The only issue in this beautiful, human world is that negativity shouts and positivity is mostly silent creating a wrong impression.
>
> Let us change it and send these positive messages loud and clear to all, especially the upcoming generations..."

"Meeting is an opportunity to think collectively through more than one brain and a number of hearts, it is a platform to transform from **ME to WE.**"

MFH – Leadership course

Be a good child, learn from parents, teachers and everybody around – *develop positive communication skills.*

Be a good parent and develop happy co-existence with your spouse. Learn to share your mind with your spouse – *develop positive communication skills.*

Be a good neighbour – co-existence and co-development of self & neighbours.

Learn to share your mind with your neighbours – *develop positive communication skills.*

Be a good support to your children – develop virtual leadership level with your children. Learn to share your mind – *develop positive communication skills.*

You are ready. You have learnt managing yourself with seniors, peers, colleagues & subordinates.

You are a leader – graduate in leadership the practical way.

> *"Plan is a flexible, upgradable guideline for tomorrow, action of today is the factual foundation on which tomorrow will stand."*

"As we move from top management to the lower levels, the management component reduces and the leadership role increases."

> **Anil's "employers' syndrome" states**
>
> "A person may have a misconception that he/she is the employer of another person. The only employer is the organization, and the entrepreneur is the first employee."

Anil's PTSC principle (progress through self-control) states that:

"The journey of progress in life, business and management is in direct relation to journey from **control** to **self-control**."

*"**Conviction and faith** are the most powerful assets in the journey of life, business and management. These are not available off-the-shelf. An individual has to develop these virtues through hard work..."*

> "The unawareness of the top management about their responsibility and accountability usually leads to mis-management and toxic culture."

"Management of leaders requires a higher level of management skills. It is important that in a group of leaders the leadership is in the right hands at the right time. It is very likely that, if not managed, the leadership will go in the hands of the louder one and not the right one."

MFH says ASK QUESTIONS IF...

"Ask question only when you are ready to ask the question...

Ask question... If you understand the question.

Ask question... If you have not predetermined the answer.

Ask question... If you really don't know the answer.

Ask question... If your intention is not to test the other person.

Ask question... If you are willing to listen.

Ask question only when you are ready to ask the question..."

> *"Keep compassion limitless and greed limited..."* **AB-MFH**

MFH on AVERAGE OR EXTREME

"We talk on averages,

We build data on averages,

But,

We always think about extremes.

Work on improving extremes, both positive and negative, averages will automatically improve."

> "Perception is a view of reality from the camera fixed at one point.
>
> On the other hand, truth is a 360 deg view. Humans are supposed to move in all directions to seek the truth, even to the other person's shoes..."

"Go for continuous improvement by continuously upgrading your self-benchmark rather than going for targets and goals."

> "Meetings should only be used for seeing & visualising the future and not for post-mortems or re-post-mortems. A platform which brings in a number of brains & hearts also brings a number of attitudes & EGOs."

MFH ON APPRECIATION

"In business & management, it is normally the other way round & that is more devastating. I know that the team member has done a great job, better than my expectations, but... I won't appreciate & pretend as if it was ordinary. I am afraid to appreciate because I assume that if I appreciate:

- He will ask for a disproportionately big favor, or
- Others will also start expecting...

I have many illogical reasons for not being appreciative."

"The biggest enemies to proper decision taking are:

1. *Attempting to please everyone through consensus building or*
2. *EGO associated with MY decision which says that decisions are irreversible."*

> "Same team member who is a 'positive contributor' in one organization, becomes a 'toxic character' in another organization. We cannot blame the person.
>
> It depends on the culture creators…"

"Leadership is not a post. It can flow from any person to any person, even to an outsider or to a remotely located person also.

It is a **situational transient responsibility**…"

MFH says

*"Meeting is an information-gathering and giving mechanism, but should be used very carefully as a **decision-taking** place."*

> "If you have taken a few steps in the wrong direction and you realise there is a better way which can make up for the extra steps, don't allow your EGO to distract you and go in for the required change."

"Never keep your team members on-the-edge. It is a mis-conception that people on-the-edge perform better. It is good once in a while and does not help in creating a good atmosphere."
AB-MFH

MFH – FAMILIES AND ORGANIZATIONS

"Families and organizations are the building blocks of the society.

Parents try to keep the morale of their kids high. They always try to give a positive atmosphere in their home.

The heads of organizations (owners, directors, heads… the top managements) are the parents for all the team members. If they also try to maintain a positive atmosphere in their organizations, this world can transform…

Most of the negativity and issues of the society start from organizations. This is the most important accountability of the managements."

"**Empathy** is not unidirectional. If it is expected that management empathizes Doers & Executors, the Doers & Executors are also required to empathize with the management. The management has to seek support from the team members to open the bridge. This will lead to a bond that will be the foundation of a great organization."

> "This is a very difficult situation I like it and the organization does not need it..."
> **AB-MFH**

"Success of an organization is based on the value it gives to the **human values & principles**; and is not based on its rules & regulations, books and discipline & system manuals."

Appreciate only if you really feel like...

*"See the good, feel the good and then appreciate the good. Never act like an appreciator. Be simple, be real, be appreciative. Appreciate as much as you **really feel**. Simple but not easy..."*

> "Organizations play a vital role in the personal life of the team members and development of society at large." **AB-MFH**

COMMUNICATION IS LIKE WATER

"Any organizational nutrient, like responsibility, accountability, opportunity, etc. absorbed by the root (the top management) can flow to all the parts of the organization tree only through the carrier water of communication..."

> *"Amongst owners, investors, vendors, customers, hired management, executors and doers, the hired management is the biggest stake holder. A contrarian belief."*

MFH on QUALITY AND TIME

"Management has to ensure that:

1. The time-oriented work is completed in time and
2. The quality-oriented work is completed as per requirement.

Most of the jobs fall under the latter, but we try to follow the methodology of the former and we land up with poor quality. If we follow the methodology of quality,w the former will automatically happen..."

> "Meeting is not a platform for responsibility sharing..." **AB-MFH**

AB-MFH simply puts
"Problem solving and Decision making are part of the process to the final event of Decision taking (DT)."

MANAGEMENT/ORGANIZATION EXPECTATION

"People are always positive and sincere towards their work, invariably. At times, they may not be aware of the expectations of the management, but they are clear about the organization's expectations."

"I am comfortable being uncomfortable,

I am uncomfortable when I am comfortable...

This happens with me, you and everybody. Everybody wants to be out of their so-called, comfort zones. Let us make the whole world – the comfort zone for our team members."

"Working is simple & good in a group if there is one leader and rest followers. The real issue crops up when there is more than one leader in a group." **AB-MFH**

> "Learn with a confidant and commit mistakes in front of your coach. Surrender to their feedbacks and rehearse mentally. Then learning from mistakes is faster and less painful."

MFH on ORDER AND CHAOS

"It is always better to move to a little distance away and take the calm, distant, preferably aerial view where you can see more threads and links. Then the decision of chaos or order is more relevant and real."

> "Dynamism does not necessarily mean always running, on your toes, it also involves recuperating, preparing and waiting patiently for the right time."

Confession of the decision taker (DT): "Many activities happen in my organization because I like them and not because the organization needs them."

> "Don't worry about committing mistakes. Learn from them. The most important key here is the coach and the confidant."

MFH urges that the process of induction of a team member should be done by the top management. The process should ensure that there is no need to resort to separation later on."

"All activities need to be directed towards the needs of the organization both short & long term, and nothing else. Personifying the organization helps in achieving this."

> "Orderly and harmonic situations often appear chaotic if you are too close or too anxious. Before accepting the situation, it is always better to confirm and re-confirm your own position of observation".

"But being harsh to others and to yourself for mistakes is not required. Mistakes are not committed, they happen, we are human. It's always better to realize, accept, learn and move on, no lingering regrets…"

MFH WARNS AGAINST FOCUS ON RULES

"Focus on the process of developing principles. Principled people follow guidelines naturally."

> **TARGETS & MANAGEMENT LETHARGY**
>
> "Managing without targets requires an active management which cannot be lethargic at all. They have to be energetic & involved. Target is for the easy-going managements who do not wish to involve themself and are happy to achieve 'X' with difficulty. They can shift their responsibility and use TARGET as a scape-goat."

"Management is comparable to 'sadhutva' or being a 'yogi', a puritan. They are the people who have dedicated their lives, their selves for the organization."

MFH - MANAGEMENT AND CO-EXISTENCE

"All our management principle makers have to understand the basic concepts of coexistence to be practical. We have to deal with the challenges of coexistence and take advantage of the benefits of coexistence.

We coexist with likes, opposites and indifference. We have to face the basic attributes of it like intra-species and inter-species competition. We have to consider predators also. We have to regard the natural laws like the survival of the fittest, the big fish eating the small fish, the survival niche, competitive exclusion, & so on.

Now management is more natural."

BREAK THE MYTH THAT "CHANGE IS UNCOMFORTABLE"

We have tuned ourselves to believe that change is unpleasant, uncomfortable, etc.

The fact is that changes are need-based requirements. We should neither be change maniacs or harbor change phobia. Our obsession with this thought that change is unpleasant and uncomfortable needs to be changed, first.

Yes.

We have to make deliberate effort, do some thinking and workout a method of making the change process interesting and comfortable. The benefits of this will fully justify the effort.

Simple but not easy...

"Let's replace competition with others with self-improvement. This has to be done against self-benchmarks. History reveals that this has given wonderful results, results better than the available best…"

> "The basic assumption that the group in the consensus team or meetings will support the final decision even out of the board room is a misleading assumption."

"That is human nature. When we taste the fruit of knowledge, our so-called comfort zones vanish and we become seekers…

Humans are seekers naturally."

> "It is great to be alone at times because you are never lonely when you are alone…"

MFH says EXPERIENCE IS PRESENT

"We don't take experience from the past by going into the past. The experience was taken when the past was present.

Experience is our possession and we can leave the past forever and live in the present…"

> "Irrespective of my capacity in my organization, if I am comfortable and if I am able to enjoy my work,
> my output,
> dedication,
> contribution,
> commitment and
> efforts are going to be the best."

MFH defines
"Retirement as a state when you start drawing joy from your work."

"Life, business and management are not about competition. Let all the competition remain in sports.

We are for interdependence & co-existence..."

> *"Trust that people always love to help. This is more than sufficient reason to seek help."* **AB-MFH**

"For guidance one needs self-awareness about the lack of competence. Accepting help is also an important requirement on the path of correction. Very true. Sometimes ego does not allow you to take help and failures become inevitable."

> *"Targets are personal, not of the organization."* **AB-MFH**

"There is no single personality trait that can be associated with great leaders, apparently. But, one thing is common, the people close to the successful leaders, their associates are invariably satisfied and happy."

> "Opportunity is not what is available every day, every now and then. Opportunity is something that comes occasionally, rarely."

MFH BELIEVES IN SELF-BENCHMARKING

"The only way to improve yourself,
the organization and
the world at large
is to stop all competition and focus on self-improvement through
self-benchmarking."

"Work energises and tension tires.

Nowadays it is very common to work for extended hours, pressure of deadlines, tension to meet the targets. I have a feeling that 'work' has reduced, and 'tensions' increased. The Executors & the Doers are more tired and less efficient. Who is responsible?

Who has to take corrective actions?

It all starts from the Top..."

> **MFH** says Be-aware: "There is always a right logic to justify every wrong."

"Opportunities come rarely and we often realise after they pass. Our EGO stops us from turning back to follow it.

Hold it.

Turn back and grab the opportunity first."

MFH ON THE, SO-CALLED, COMFORT ZONE

"The word comfort zone is a misnomer.

The, so-called, comfort zone of a person is practically the necessities and needs of their family. People can forego their personal success, development and improvement for the sake of the comfort of their families. If the organization takes care of the family responsibilities of the team members, the team members will have an extended area of operations and unlimited operation zone."

> "Human brain is able to distinguish failure and success. It propels us towards success and away from failures. That's how all successful people have worked and achieved, it is no rocket science."

MFH says

"The most important factor in the battle of doubt and faith is that even 0.1% doubt is heavy on 99.9% faith. Zero doubt, 100% faith is the requirement…"

> **MFH** WARNS AGAINST VERTICAL COMPETITION
>
> "Competition of any type is dangerous for the organization, nevertheless the worst condition arises when an organization is faced with vertical competition.
>
> Does vertical competition exist?
>
> Definitely yes.
>
> It is the most dangerous form of competition."

"Let us re-think and re-work to reduce tension to increase productivity…"

"When we talk of life, business and management, consistency should always come before creativity. Management is primarily a dish of consistency flavored with seasoning of creativity." **AB-MFH**

> "We are fascinated by big cupboards having apparels which we are never going to use.
>
> We are trying to collect much more data, information, so-called-knowledge (unnecessary junk) in the name of competition & growth. This is adding to the time wasters of our team members and we are responsible for it."

"We should refrain from attempting to draw a workable strategy for life, business and management from war or sports analogies."

"We have to

- Do festival cleaning of our minds and
- Stop garbage collection.

It's time to ask, 'Does my organization really need it' before taking any data or acquiring any system."

> "The facilities available today should have reduced the load on humans, but the facts are contrary to the expectations. Organizations need to shed their 'time wasters' and drastically & ruthlessly cut the work hours without cutting remuneration. Productivity will shoot up..."

"You don't need to be a master, just go for the spectators view and you will get the right perspective..."

> *"The natural way to make anything perennial is to make it cyclic..."* **AB-MFH**

"The conclusion is that by trying to be independent we are attempting impossible. We are seeking something un-natural."

> "It is not important as to how many times I have to follow. It is important that I must follow till the desired result is achieved."

MFH ASKS THE TEAM LEADERS TO SHOW SUCCESS:

"As a team leader, we have to show small successes in the direction of the bigger one. This not only keeps the team engaged, it also helps in keeping them together and in high spirits."

"No doubt money is important, but more than money it is the status associated with money that sustains the motivation."

> **MFH** - A VERY TYPICAL PROBLEM
>
> "I want that I should take all the decisions but the team members should be responsible for those decisions...
>
> The management."

"I & No, are the two smallest words in the vocabulary. Both are very dangerous, but the latter is more critical as it relieves the user from answerability and responsibility shifting onus on the person saying YES."

> *"Humans always want to make things easy..."*
> **AB-MFH**

"Once I develop faith in my concept, I work to reach a state of conviction and all the so-called problems vanish in thin air..."

AB-MFH

> **MFH** says
> "Learning is not
> reading, writing or listening.
> Learning is awareness and acquiring.
> It is all about implementation."

"Perception is verifiable by opening our eyes, entering other person's shoes & using required tools. Let us stop hiding behind perceptions & face the truth."

> "The most inefficient is a bunch of leaders who cannot transfer leadership to one person at a time..."

- To my parents who gave me to the world.
- My wife who gave me re-birth.
- My children who guided me during my mental travel from Gen X to Gen Z.
- Various organizations where I worked who made me what I am.

- To all persons whom I met as they all taught me something new every time.
- To all writers who shared their experiences and understandings.
- Thankyou GOD (Brahma Vishnu Mahesh...)

www.ingramcontent.com/pod-product-compliance
Lightning Source LLC
Chambersburg PA
CBHW020920180526
45163CB00007B/2815